D1629590

THE LITTLE BOOK OF
DANNY DYER

The wit and wisdom
of the **diamond geezer**

THE LITTLE BOOK OF
DANNY DYER

The wit and wisdom
of the **diamond geezer**

A CIP catalogue record for this book is
available from the British Library.

ISBN (Hardback) 978 1 4091 9293 0
ISBN (eBook) 978 1 4091 9294 7

Printed in Italy

MIX
Paper from
responsible sources
FSC® C023419
FSC
www.fsc.org

www.orionbooks.co.uk

CONTENTS

POLITICS

'WE ARE LIVING IN AN AGE OF FOOD BANKS. HOW THE F*CK DID THAT HAPPEN? SERIOUSLY.'

THE BIG ISSUE

19 November 2018

'YOU WATCH *QUESTION*
NO ONE KNOWS WHAT
MAD RIDDLE.'

TIME, IT'S COMEDY.
T IS. IT'S LIKE THIS

ON BREXIT, *GOOD EVENING, BRITAIN*
28 June 2018

'WHAT'S HAPPENED TO THAT
ON? . . . HOW COME HE CAN
HE'S IN EUROPE, IN NICE WITH
HE SHOULD BE HELD

TWAT CAMERON WHO BROUGHT IT
SCUTTLE OFF? . . . **WHERE IS HE?**
HIS TROTTERS UP. . . I THINK
ACCOUNTABLE FOR IT.'

ON BREXIT, *GOOD EVENING, BRITAIN*
28 June 2018

'I THOUGHT IT WAS COMMON KNOWLEDGE THAT DAVID CAMERON IS A F*CKING TWAT.'

LOOK BACK TO THE FUTURE,
17 December 2018

'THE POLITICIANS HAVE ALL BEEN EXPOSED AS INADEQUATE PEOPLE THAT TALK S**T CONSTANTLY.'

THE BIG ISSUE
19 November 2018

'I MEAN, WHERE ARE
WHERE ARE THEY?
BACKSTABBING THAN

OUR LEADERS?
THERE'S BEEN MORE
WE HAVE IN
ALBERT SQUARE!'

CHANNEL 4'S ALTERNATIVE CHRISTMAS MESSAGE
25 December 2018

'HE'S JUST OFF HIS NUT,
THIS GEEZER. HE'S A CARTOON.
YOU JUST SIT BACK AND GO,
"HOW THE F*CKING HELL HAS
THAT HAPPENED?"'

ON DONALD TRUMP, *THE LAST LEG*
8 December 2017

'YOU VOTED FOR THE CONSERVATIVES, SO DO US A FAVOUR AND VOTE FOR *EASTENDERS*, IF YOU FANCY IT [AT THE SOAP AWARDS].'

THE PAUL O'GRADY SHOW
20 April 2015

FAMILY

'THIS IS *UNIVERSITY CHALLENGE*. SOME WOULD SAY MAYBE I COULD HAVE SENT YOU DOWN THAT ROUTE: UNIVERSITY.'

TO DANI DYER,
GOGGLEBOX: CELEBRITY SPECIAL
18 November 2019

'I'M SWEET WITH HIM

NEVER DROPS FROM

AS LONG AS A TEAR

HER F*CKING EYE.'

ON HIS DAUGHTER'S POTENTIAL BOYFRIENDS,
BACKCHAT WITH JACK WHITEHALL AND HIS DAD
20 November 2013

'I WANT TO GIVE MY CHILDREN
EVERYTHING THAT I DIDN'T HAVE.'

***HELLO* MAGAZINE**

29 January 2019

'I TEACH MY GIRLS THEY CAN
BE WHO THEY WANT TO BE, AND
I TRY AND TEACH MY BOY TO
BE A GOOD MAN.'

CHANNEL 4'S ALTERNATIVE CHRISTMAS MESSAGE
25 December 2018

'IT'S ALL ABOUT

LOVE AND AFFECTION

IN MY FAMILY.'

THE ONE SHOW
31 January 2019

'I CAN'T MOAN AS A FATHER,
SHE HASN'T PUT A FOOT WRONG,
ME AND MY WIFE ARE LIKE
PARENTS OF THE YEAR.'

ON HIS DAUGHTER DANI DYER,
GOOD EVENING, BRITAIN
28 June 2018

'I WAS A BABY WHEN I HAD DANI – I COULDN'T EVEN SHAVE.'

HELLO MAGAZINE

29 January 2019

ROYALTY

'I'VE GOT SCROLLS COMING OUT
OF ME EARHOLES.'

DANNY DYER'S RIGHT ROYAL FAMILY

23 January 2019

'I THINK I'M GOING TO TREAT MYSELF TO A RUFF. JUST GET A MASSIVE RUFF AND BOWL ABOUT WITH IT AND IF ANYONE QUESTIONS IT THEN I'LL EXPLAIN TO THEM WHY I'M WEARING A RUFF.'

WHO DO YOU THINK YOU ARE?

24 November 2016

'I LIKE TO EMBRACE EVERY HISTORIAN WITH A BIG CUDDLE AT THE BEGINNING, YOU KNOW, TO MAKE THEM SETTLE DOWN, AND JUST HAVE AN OLD CHINWAG ABOUT MEDIEVAL HISTORY.'

PRESS ASSOCIATION

14 January 2019

'I JUST HAVE TO DIGEST
MY NUT AND THEN

THIS AND **GET THIS IN**
CAN MOVE ON WITH
MY LIFE.'

ON FINDING OUT HE'S DESCENDED FROM ROYALTY,
WHO DO YOU THINK YOU ARE?
24 November 2016

'I'VE NEVER BEEN ON A HORSE
IN MY LIFE BUT I WAS GALLOPING
AND EVERYTHING.'

THE ONE SHOW
31 January 2019

'I DO LOVE A MOAT, ME.'

DANNY DYER'S RIGHT ROYAL FAMILY

23 January 2019

'WELL, BASICALLY

'M ROYALTY.

**ALAN CARR'S NEW YEAR
SPECSTACULAR**

31 December 2016

'HE CAME FROM A SLUM, I COME FROM A SLUM.'

ON HIS CONNECTION WITH HIS ANCESTOR THOMAS CROMWELL, *RADIO TIMES*

14 November 2016

'IT'S JUST STUPID REALLY TO THINK
I'M RELATED TO KINGS AND A SAINT.'

THE ONE SHOW
31 January 2019

'WHERE'S ME

CRAHN?!

DANNY DYER'S RIGHT ROYAL FAMILY

23 January 2019

'IF THEY ARE STRUGGLING TO FIND A KING, I'M YOUR MAN!'

THE BIG ISSUE

24 November 2018

'I'M ROYALTY THAT'S GONE WRONG.'

**ALAN CARR'S NEW YEAR
SPECSTACULAR**
31 December 2016

LIFE

'I DON'T THINK YOU SHOULD BE
ABLE TO HAVE SLUSH PUPPIES
WHEN YOU WANT, I THINK IT
SHOULD BE A TREAT.'

THE JONATHAN ROSS SHOW
31 October 2015

'DO NOT LET WHERE
DEFINE WHERE YOU'RE
BE WHOEVER

YOU'VE COME FROM
GOING IN LIFE. YOU CAN
YOU WANT TO BE.

NATIONAL TELEVISION AWARDS 2019
22 January 2019

'I'VE BECOME QUITE SPIRITUAL.
I BELIEVE THERE'S A HIGHER
POWER LOOKING AFTER ME.'

I NEWS

6 February 2019

'I WAS ALLOWED FOUR "F*CKS", I GOT THEM OUT THE WAY EARLY DOORS.'

ON HIS APPEARANCE ON
HAVE I GOT NEWS FOR YOU, I NEWS
6 February 2019

'I LIVE BY TWO RULES: NOURISH

CURB YOUR **EGO**,
YOUR **SOUL**.'

NATIONAL TELEVISION AWARDS 2019
22 January 2019

'WHAT IS ART? A LOT OF PEOPLE ASK THIS QUESTION AND I'M HAPPY TO BE ABLE TO CLEAR IT UP ONCE AND FOR ALL. ART IS SOMETHING THAT GETS YOU BY THE B*LLOCKS.'

**THE WORLD ACCORDING TO DANNY DYER:
LIFE LESSONS FROM THE EAST END**
22 October 2015

'I GOT TWO RIGHT. SOMETIMES
I FRIGHTEN MYSELF WITH THE
KNOWLEDGE I'VE GOT ACTUALLY.'

ON *UNIVERSITY CHALLENGE,*
GOGGLEBOX: CELEBRITY SPECIAL
18 November 2019

'LOVELY GAFF.'

ON THE MIDDLE EAST,
LOOK BACK TO THE FUTURE
17 December 2018

'I WAS SURROUNDED BY WOMEN WHO DIDN'T STOP RABBITING ON.'

ON GROWING UP, *LOOSE WOMEN*
24 November 2015

'IT'S HANDY, A BIT O'
GO OUT AND **VACUUM**

ASTRO. JUST HAVE TO
IT OCCASIONALLY.'

ON TWITTER, *GUARDIAN*
21 November 2013

'WHAT DO YOU NEED IN A PUB? BEER PUMPS, A BAR, LINO, A DART BOARD AND A POOL TABLE. MAYBE A TELLY FOR THE FOOTBALL. CHAIRS AND TABLES, CLEARLY. MAYBE A BEER TOWEL FOR COLOUR. THAT'S IT.'

THE WORLD ACCORDING TO DANNY DYER:
LIFE LESSONS FROM THE EAST END
22 October 2015

'IF YOUR BIN GETS CHAWED AND YOU RING THE COUNCIL AND ASK THEM FOR A BIN, YOU'VE GOT MORE CHANCE OF THEM COMING AROUND AND FITTING A JACUZZI IN YOUR HOUSE.'

THE JONATHAN ROSS SHOW

31 November 2015

'FAME IS

GRAFT.

ALAN CARR: CHATTY MAN
20 November 2015

'I SWEAR I'VE SEEN ONE, ON VIDEO.'

ON ALIENS, *ALAN CARR: CHATTY MAN*
20 November 2015

'IT'S A RIGHT NUTTY NIGHT. LAST YEAR
I ENDED UP LICKING MARY BERRY.'

TV CHOICE AWARDS 2018
10 September 2018

'I THINK I GET THIS HARDMAN
IMAGE, WHICH IS UNFAIR. I'M
A SENSITIVE LITTLE SOUL REALLY,
QUITE A SPIRITUAL MAN AS WELL.'

PRESS ASSOCIATION
14 January 2019

'IT TAKES US A LONG TIME TO
GROW UP AS MEN.'

SUN
27 December 2018

'I DON'T REALLY WANT TO

SO **LET'S**

GIVE HER ANY OXYGEN

JOG HER ON.'

ON KATIE HOPKINS, *THE PAUL O'GRADY SHOW*
20 April 2015

'I THINK YOUR CLUB CHOOSES YOU.
YOU DON'T CHOOSE YOUR CLUB.'

ON FOOTBALL, *ME AND MY CLUB*
9 April 2014

'I DON'T WANT TO BE KNOWN AS A HARDMAN EVEN. I DON'T UNDERSTAND IT. MAYBE IT'S THE WAY I TALK. OR THE FACT I SWEAR A LOT.'

PRESS ASSOCIATION
9 April 2013

'JUST FUCKING BLANK GET THE

THEM. **NUT DOWN**,

BLOWER OUT.'

ON FANS, *ALAN CARR: CHATTY MAN*
20 November 2015

'IF YOU'RE BLAGGING IT AS AN ACTOR, YOU'LL BE EXPOSED ONCE YOU COME INTO A SOAP. THAT'S WHAT I'D SAY TO THE SNOBBY MOB.'

RADIO TIMES

12 May 2014

'GRAFT YOUR B*LLOCKS OFF.'

ALAN CARR: CHATTY MAN
20 November 2015

'MY BUM IS FLAPPING A LITTLE BIT.'

DANNY DYER'S DEADLIEST MEN
20 October 2008

'I SAY WHAT I THINK AND I GET
RESPECTED FOR IT OR I GET
ASSASSINATED FOR THAT.'

ON TWITTER, *GUARDIAN*
20 November 2013

'I DON'T EAT BREAKFAST,' SAYS THE OLD LADY TO HER PONY. **COFFEE,**

ME. A COFFEE AND

SNOUT, PONY.

THE BIG ISSUE
24 November 2018

'I THINK FEMINISM HAS BEEN
A GREAT THING FOR MEN.'

LOOSE WOMEN
24 November 2015

'*COUNTRYFILE* DID MAKE ME
CRY ONCE WHEN A LAMB DIDN'T
MAKE IT. I GET VERY EMOTIONAL
ABOUT THINGS.'

RADIO TIMES
12 May 2014

'I'M GOING TO BE STRAIGHT WITH YOU NOW. I'VE HAD A BIT OF A LATE ONE, I FEEL A BIT ROPEY, SO I HOPE HE TAKES IT NICE AND EASY ON ME.'

AS SOMEONE IS ABOUT TO SHOOT HIM,
DANNY DYER'S DEADLIEST MEN

20 October 2008

'I THOUGHT I SHOULD DO
SOMETHING PRE-WATERSHED
FOR ONCE IN ME LIFE.'

THE JONATHAN ROSS SHOW
1 February 2014

'NOW, DON'T GET ME

SAINT, YOU KNOW, I CAM

WE CAM

WRONG, I AIN'T NO
DO BETTER. I THINK
ALL DO BETTER.'

ANNEL 4'S ALTERNATIVE CHRISTMAS MESSAGE
25 December 2018

'WHEN YOU HAVE A BIT OF FAME,
YOU HAVE A RESPONSIBILITY
TO SPEAK UP'

SUN
27 December 2018

'DON'T TRY TO BE TOO CLEVER.'

THE PAUL O'GRADY SHOW
11 November 2009

'I DUNNO IF I'D USE FULL STOPS TO
BE HONEST WITH YOU.'

ON TEXT MESSAGING,
MICHAEL MCINTYRE'S BIG SHOW
25 November 2017

'DON'T TAKE YOURSELF
TOO SERIOUSLY.'

THE PAUL O'GRADY SHOW
11 November 2009